when feelin
fully at hon
in the driftii
living room
of time

:

poems

jim ferguson

Acknowledgments

Some of these poems have appeared in the following on-line and/or paper publications: *Anything Anymore Anywhere, Common Sense, Air, Edinburgh Review, West Coast Magazine, New Writing Scotland, The Echo Room, Harry's Hand, Gutter, The Treacle Well, The Wide Skirt, Scratch, Mutter Shutter, Jacket2, Nerve, Rat's Ass Review, Raums, The Curly Mind, More than Quirky (cd)*. And in the pamphlets titled *Acts of Fiction, Songs to Drown a Million Souls, Dark Afore Nine, Fugitive Bullets, My Bonnie Scotland* and *Strong Drink*. Thanks to the editors.

CONTENTS

2

night-music

back
when you were growing

nothing
kept you down,

***

huge chunks of grief spill from the heart,
carousel cradle of night rolls over
drowns in a river of sleep that buries,
numbs and cures all there is to be cured:

fixed and repaired with all debts paid,
one last savage duty for dignity in life
for all that is dear, close to the soul,
blood-tied love in a watery grave,

grief torn hearts
                              sentimental journeys

***

no monsters out the walls today
no madness muckle scotch whisky shit
something still behind the eyes but
small dots crawling insect style
in the forefront of the brain

***

now there is no more waiting
there is nothing clever left
to put in words on a page
a savage wind battered
all the life out

life in   life out
        shake it

        light

                        a floating sense

***

who says there is no inner life?
the dull trouble with dusting
and producing clean clothes
to wear for no real reason

those unkempt types have it right
still you have to snatch a balance,
a big beam of balance, and squares
and mathematical symbols —

no really
                        naw
                                        no awright

know
                know what?
                                jesus christ   free will

                watch for the tide

coming in   come on in

                sudden and bright

***

away you go
sailing out
i don't know

that sentiment isn't all right
nothing is all right
everything is fine

***

as if in the exercise of free will
you'd go on a journey, a stupefying voyage
in addition to the daily life
the life aye, dilly-dally back n forth

worried about weans and housework
as bold a sacred everyday joy as any
has the right to ask for
that's possibly that   that's   that
                                                      that
                                                   that-that

***

rattled and raw we were but still dancing
to a tune long dead, but sure we were sure
it would scream once again on the airwaves
over motorways and mountains whizz around

the global village knapsack intact
HEY! look at our eyes now
smiling into a sea of adversity
ready to surf to the auld rhythmic tune made anew

***

now you are in network heaven
network heaven made from spectacle glue
broken cups and used tea-bags
                (DIY cyber-heid) noo that yir deid
this is what we do

                                    in   out

in out, in out,   shake it all about
                      shake it all
                      shake it
about you

it's about you, me and everybody else
who knows us in network-land(?)

                      hang-up
                      log-off
                      power-down
                      de-boot

shoot mamma   *cool* ("in americana")

                          cool holyrood blues

take the bus to edinburgh

                          search for your roots

***

done
finished
finally
undone
but ready
for something

remarkably
new born

***

switch on the radio

night-music
                                    sleep

                        morning

switch off the radio

        go back

                                                let us

go   back

                            n forward

LIFE EXPECTANCY

because i
expect to be
alive
in 2 weeks

time   even   still
i always delay
opening
any book i buy
for a
regulation
fortnight

though

i know
by writing this

i'm
tempting fate

BATTERED AULD CLOCK

kicked doon the street
face aw smashed in
nae legs tae staun oan

hauns bent oota shape
nuthin tae say
nae ane tae tell
o the good times —

the miracle is: you are ticking
the miracle is: you are ticking

*

battered old clock
kicked down the street
face all smashed in
no legs to stand on

hands bent out of shape
nothing to say
no one to tell
of the good times

the miracle is: you are ticking
the miracle is: you are ticking

John Wayne Can't Jump that Hedge Because he's Dead

bleach —
bleach just kills stuff

humans
shouldn't drink it

or use it
too much

*

over a million
mini-white-moths

can live inside
your vacuum cleaner

*

bacteria —
mostly too small to see

even if you've had a recent eye-test

but
they like to live in your gut

and in yogurt

*

two kinds of people

those with passports
and those without

*

the counting of syllables
    exact same thing as

    the measuring of skulls
are there really poetry fascists?

*

The apostrophe hang-up
a new mental illness

*

some chairs
are too expensive

to burn
when you're cold

*

advanced artificial intelligence
that just kills stuff

dumb artificial intelligence
a great humanitarian tool

drone drone drone

*

footballers wages
and transfer fees

loose change
for any pensioner

*

two kinds of people

the rich
and the rest

*

why do thousands
obey a few who have guns

why do the few with guns
mostly work for the rich

*

why are some ponies
immune to the midgie

*

no one invented DNA

was it always there

*

blind empiricism
can make your nose bleed

*

bleach and bacteria —
the natural inhabitants

of the toilet bowl

*

open sewers
have a natural tendency to riot

*

toilet humour —
best appreciated by the lower orders

*

the suppression of the urge to happiness
is good for your health

god has told us this
via many prophets and faiths

god knows
what he's doing

*

the inventor of spaghetti has stated

the truly uncivilised
eat their main course
with a fork and spoon

*

Harry doesn't like dogs
although he is one

*

the Nietzschean aphorism
is by no means a vehicle

for driving
philosophical inquiry

*

comparing tomatoes with bananas
is by no means a vehicle

for driving
an analogy home

*

how does an olive know
where Israel is

when it can't even jump
over the wall

*

the inventor of the spoon has stated

this is not a tool
to be used in the fight against fascism

*

John Wayne can't jump that hedge because he's dead.

5 POEMS ON THE ORDINARINESS OF LIFE
AT THE OUTSET OF THE NINETEEN NINETIES

garden maintenance

they're hacking the trees in the park
hacking them back

like america in its own backyard
mowing them down with automatic weapons

in arenas where the grass is short
where weak top-soil is strengthened by blood

they're hacking the trees in the park
like the western world is teaching iraq

hacking them back
getting things into line

giving people death and disease
for their own good

it's better to be murdered and bombed
than suffer the rule of any dictator

they're hacking the trees
to let them flourish

or to stop
the communist poison spreading

and it's just
helping nature along the way

like napalm adds fuel to the fire

of searing flesh

and they're hacking the bodies back in the park
so they're just the right size

to fit in mass graves
and we'll be told about that

when it's in the interests of
good government

under the stars

weeping

on the cold mountain top
the weather is not as bad as expected

but not good enough
to keep the frail

from turning to cold
blue flesh

not good enough
to put a roof overhead

not good enough
to remain undead

kurdistan murdered
by explosives and diplomacy

<u>making the trains run on time</u>

in the western world calm as any contented lamb
government and business go on unabated
with a citizens' charter to bring down the unions
legislating individuals out of the collective

in the western world with everything silent
roses recline on the drawing room table
the security men at the patio door
with chicken wings and barbecue sauce

thick and dark as the blood for oil
oil-barons staying home to relax
the soldiers being sent out to roost
in the heat and hell without air-conditioning

they'll get the trains to run on time while
scientists and missionaries tug their forelocks
bow before the meaning of money
and endless demands of the market economy

diplomats sleep in the best hotels
deliver the skills of administration
serving up the interests of oil
claiming the credit for making the "peace"

they fire their paper guns
and cruise missiles land a few streets away
in the best spirit of Hollywood movies
Presidents and Prime Ministers say,

go ahead, make my day!

here, have a beer from the fridge
ain't you glad you don't live in the desert
they roast in daylight and freeze in the dark
cheers, here's to our boys out there

we'll have to keep teaching the arabs a lesson
then we'll show them how
to make trains run on time
we'll show them the meaning of democracy

in the western world calm as any contented lamb
business and government go on unabated
sheep graze peacefully on the hillsides
high above lochs and the geiger counters

the Good Shepherd is watching over the flock
the Good Shepherd is always male
the Good Shepherd is always wise
the Good Shepherd provides guidance for the west

scream

today

the torturer wears a white suit and canvas shoes

very casual
as on the mountain the cold kills
indoors the heat is terror and pain

scream.

ordinary days

these are ordinary days
no boundaries to the horror and shock
a fucking laugh if ever there was one
the underlying violence in the metaphor

in the blinding solitude of the sands
the grains slipping through eye sockets
slipping through earholes, mouth, nostrils
filling our skulls with burning quartz

burning out the nerve ends of wisdom and age
burning out the nerve ends of youth
bringing on the never ending war and despair
and misery at not being able to stop it. here
                                        at
                                        this

                                        full-stop.

always these days never now

always these days
seem to feel the cold

seeming to feel the cold
seem or seeming?

sometime back
in summer's dreaming

i didn't feel the cold
at all

*

like Alexander
young and spritely

twenty mile a day by bicycle
rain or shine, all weathers mind ye

healthily back n forth
until his breath stopped

working everyday
the way it did before

when he was moving well
always those days

going fast downhill
through time's crossroads

there it was
seems like

it
was

there always
not there

now

*

if not feeling the cold
having a cold

having or feeling?

chemtrail symptoms
conspiracy theories

from somewhere high
the aeroplanes

release molecular junk

*

very carefully
considering

the order
of release

of the words
out of the mouth

if not the mouth
the mind

mouth or mind?

indeed
the arrangement

of lines
on the page

— what is a page —
the screen's dimensions

screen or paper?

*

buried the pains of history
inside an abstract box
and called it all nostalgia

we were, they said,
suffering from melancholia

*

there is an inference
that can't be detected

back and forward
neural messages

form of semaphore -/-
imperceptible brain activity

when you are doing
what you are doing

you don't know
why you're doing it

there are machines
to help us see inside

the consciousness
that eludes us

*

afeared of the fascism
contained within

imperial nationalisms —
we dreamt of a world government

with limited powers
and badly run

to which we could subscribe
and circumscribe big business

until we could castrate
the global market

all
together

without pain
without nostalgia

*

the year zero
seemed

too far
back in the mist

of time
for us

to travel
there —

instead
we let

the ice-
caps

m

e

l

t

... --- ...   .

and went there anyway

    *

       utter
      absurd
    get more
       from
     nothing

       than
    actually
         is

 *

get more
do more
say more

everything
always

ever e x pa n d i   n   g

*

ever expanding
colossal growth
from finite resources

impossible algorithms
churning forevers
for endless consumption

*

registers
for cash
and language

*

at the top
a plethora

of

profusions:

the bottom
left

without
stuff of life

can't be made
from a dollar a day

kind of industry

*

thank god
for electronic cash transfers

make your mark out of interest
nothing is something

*

every sweet
brings magic

*

check the equations

*

—trigger ... ear
sounds of violence

face on the ground
forces you down

into a hole
to dig our gems

from out the dross
left without even

your dollar a day
it's transferred interest

it's off and away
what cash? what language?

cash or language?
bellowing babies

with swollen bellies
swallow air

feed the mystical soul
of gaping capital

*

interest
interest

interest
interest

interest
interest

intersat
money

transferred
up

*

liquid
security

take your contingency
into the army

all is opaque
blood and oil

federal reserve
is a very very very fine wine

*

metal moves
at incredible speed

through flesh and bone —
nothing to see

hear
touch or taste

witnesses mute
can't even moan

or
make tiny

   sounds

                       resembling

     human

*

sweet little eyeballs
rest on the road

they squish underfoot
as onward we walk

*

skin only fit
   for the making of clothes
   that never will be

*

never feel
exquisite touch

sandpaper
tongue

lungs
of
phlegm

are we there yet?

no teeth
no gums
no mouth to eat

are we there yet?

sharing
the torture   of melancholia
         o
         f

         h
         i
         s
         t
         o
         r
         y
   of cash
     over
language

of digital
victory

stuck beside truths
we could not face

we took photos instead
checked them out later

yes it was true
we were human

*

are we dead yet ...

Berlin Shots

a sequential poem in 12 episodes

jim ferguson

we next saw the sun

i paid the men
and they sealed
the deal by enclosing us

in a metal container

we were welded
tight shut
with just water and air

and darkness

hours past
until we next saw the sun
when i found we were in

the city of berlin

into the dark

absolutely
love impossible
here or anywhere

empty street
full of wild
graffiti –

dancing before you
incredible writing
in a language

from a different planet –
what does it mean
strange streetlife

from the heart
of the addict –
slip quietly

into a nightclub
which once was a church
now completely detached

from its own nature –
a soul destroyed
cast into the desert

without boots or clothes –
and naked
behind a mirror

sits the essence

of beauty –
watch for the humans

they're rough and ready
a jumble of smiles
and a rag-bag of frowns –

see them all bankrupt
in night's endless sands –
walk into the dark

the future holds promise

nothing much
of the old wall
        left

just a few lumps to sell
to tired drunk tourists
who'd do much better

to visit the zoo –
or just take the bus
like a carousel

that spins round
and around
schönefeld airport –

angry taxi drivers
shake raging fists
at this bus

which steals
most
of their business –

and even while
they rant and rave
they still form a queue

and wait
for the suits
from business class

who don't like
the bus
and don't like to travel

in circles –
for these are the men
for whom

the future
holds
promise

waiting to forget

point to the menu
and out pops
sausage   potatoes and cabbage

'ein beer bitta'
and drink it all up
with a friendly smile

the waitress
half glides   half stomps
around the room

talking and laughing
and taking
orders from right left and centre

what is to become
of these
afternoon diners

who wait impatiently
for their food to arrive
who wait impatiently

for the fußball to start
who wait impatiently
for the barber

to arrive
- and trim their moustache
- and shave off their hair

- and drill a hole
in their head
to suck out

their brains –
while they're
staring ahead

with mouths open wide –
waiting to forget
their history

41

litres or shots

despite the snow
no one is skiing
here in berlin

at this time of year
it's usually warmer
but even london

is colder with
weather weirdness
creeping all over

northern europe –
can't explain
the change

in the sky line
above the clouds
a sea of white

upside down
mountains
say 'danke' und 'morgen'

and the beer
is
blonde

and the rum
is
cuban

and in kruezberg
welshmen
are arm-wrestling

all through the chaos
of ludicrous dreams
where freedom

rests its head
amid the wandering tribes
asking
'what measures does liberty come in, litres or shots?'

bread can sustain you

caught
in a pizza joint
on kaiser allee

busy
with broken
girls and boys

on the 4 a.m. trance –
we don't say much
but it's cold again

yes
it's cold again –
the free race by

with wheels
on their feet
and muscular legs

that can
make your nose bleed –
but we just stand and nibble

at the edge
of a giant
pizza planet –

our
knees
never bend –

while angels
are dreaming
of incredible flight

bread
can sustain you
inside and out

through
the watery air
of the night

your german eyes

i saw
      in your
      eyes

an x-ray through
to the back of my skull
bright and wonder-filled

plans of tomorrow –
your arms   your hands
your fingers   your smile

together with mine
in the kitchen
cooking big pots

of lentil soup
with potatoes
and parsnips

to keep out the cold –
one day
together

we'd grow old –
weather wild
and weather strange

what games
we'd play –
canasta and scrabble –

take deep breaths
stop our hearts
so nothing could ever unravel

or time-travel backwards
under the stairs
to where

our children would play
chinese whispers –
and inside their laughter

we knew
this was what
our love had made –

i looked in your eyes
your german eyes
in your beautiful german eyes

while you
picked my pockets
my heart   my bones –

and all exposed –
my dreams
sweet and bitter

vanished
into
the night

let it all go

sleep
why don't you –
don't walk around

on
long sad platforms
without any trains –

find a place
to lie down
take off your boots

don't mind
the looks
on the faces

of stranded
companions –
swing

from the girders
on a flying trapeze
without any net

get to land safely
on the head
of a snowman –

socks soaking wet
but
no complaints

there's no where
to walk –
no destination

and nobody waiting
with arms open wide –
keep your eyes open

dissolve in the mirror –
sleep
why don't you   let it all go

alien air

suddenly
        this
                realisation

that
you're far deeper
down
than you think

you're deep underground –
while up above
people are walking   living –
smiling or frowning

or chatting with loved ones
or hunting their enemies
or wondering where the next
meal will come from –

and you are down here
and other people are down here too
waiting to be briskly moved
from one part of the world

to another –
from one part of their lives
to another –
and all the time

they're pumping in oxygen
to keep us all going
– officials in uniform give dubious
guidance in the fine art

of travel – down here
i don't know anyone
and i wonder which station
i'm allowed to get off at

and suddenly
there are thousands
and thousands of starlings
flying in swarms

above our heads
where everything happens
without rhyme or reason –
i yearn for the surface

search for my breath
- invisible -
caught here – in the alien air
so far below

northern tundra

we asked –
could we bring
our sense of humour with us

which was different
and funnier
than yours –

'no'
we were told
you

don't like
that stuff here –
don't laugh

you told us
work hard
and we'd be fine –

but without laughter
our lives were blighted –
we had lost our voices –

lost our tongues
on the ice
of a northern tundra

the desolate end of an unknown street

i have to say –
we don't
look how we did

when we were
younger –
too many

sunset shadows
past away
beyond our eyes –

in time's dreamworld
we looked on intently
with only

youth's stupidity
as our guide –
our parents dead

along with some
contemporaries –
who fell

too early
trying to 'kiss
the sky' –

but such a
kissing game
was not for us

we did not
drive too fast
nor climb so high –

the hours
came and went
as months and years

and we stood
gently
stretching out our hands –

to get aboard
a bus whose
muddled movements

went beyond
the boundaries
of our knowing –

our arms   our hands
they withered
then they

drooped –
until Spring rains
stormed down

and washed us over
to the desolate end
of an unknown silent street –

which appears
as filled with nothing
and with plenty

the old meals
of our culture
sit half-cooked –

our hunger
now
has left us

we
no longer
beg
to eat

when will the truth meet the truth

many papers are false
but existence is real
when will the truth

meet the truth

citizens of nowhere
workers of the world
'the wrong kind of migrants'

human beings

STRONG DRINK

'You'll no doubt say
You are innocent. The damp patch
On the wall of our flats
Tells the same story.'

From, "A Worker's Speech to a Doctor"
by Bertolt Brecht.

no luv

am on thi broo
but ma shoodirs ir wide
give us that burden
let mi carry that burden
let mi pay ma ain way
though ahv nae fuckin money

cummon ya bastards
give mi thi burden
canny manage thinoo
wahnti manage less n less

ah wahnti bi skint
ah wahnt that burden uv poverty
ah luv fuckin poverty
ah luv bein poor

cummon give us mer
give us mern fuckin mern fuckin
pile on thi misery
give mi beans n toast
fur ma tea ivry night

&

ah hear yi on thi news
sayn aye itsawright
them poor wans
dont wahnti bi molicoddled
fuckin molicoddled

smuthird in motherly luv
ir faitherly luv
ir any kinda luv
ir that State Paternalism

give mi thi burden
ma shoodirs ir wide
n ma heids beef

but ma dinnir isny

next they'll be reading poetry

jist whit is it they wahnti see?
moanin aboota tenner fur an eye test

ahl show thi bastards a thing ur two,
jist wait ti they wahnt an operation

scottish homes

see whin yivgoat dampness
nyi canny give up smokin

fucks yi   so it does

arse

- yi needti kick sum arse

coz thats whit am here fur
ti kick arse

n if you dont kick their arses
then am gawny kick yours

thats thi way it goes
hierarchical structures intit

n am at thi top
so get kickin,

art/empire

uch aye
ah getyi noo
whityi wur sayn aboot
thi unimployd n that

ah get whityi mean
but it wiz thi way yi put it
it wiz thi way yi said it
it almost

it wiz almost
a r t i s t i c

thi optimist

no sense n talkin aw that shite
aboot urban alienation
n faceless bureaucracy

get right outyir box

thats better isnt it

blow

YIR DEALINWI AN UNEXPLODEDMAN

am gonny go aff

like a bad egg

am smelly
ahno am smelly

so fuck off nsniff sumbdy else

mood elevation

thir wiz sum lovely blue pills
thir wizza landin pad fur space junk
thir wizzan empty shaft
wi nae box ti take yi back doon

nwhit goes
must come
n vice-versa

thir wizza loata cummin n gawn

spinnin

yi get that spinnin sensation
like whinyi stawn up too fast

thi flair dizny feel solid unnir yir feet anymer
strange so it is

then yir sweatn like an athlete
nyi wish yi wur an athlete nsteedia newrotic

yi wish ti god sumhn somewhere wid happn
that makes yi feel like yi mean sumhn

a miracle ur such like

but its aw jist thi same
same heid   same body

same ivrihin else
face nthi mirra.etc.

thi deception

remembir that burd
wi thi massive jugs

that came up ti yir flat
a cuppla yearago steamin

n wheeched aff ir jersey
n ther they wur bouncin

aw wobbly

ah seenir jist thi othir day
walkin by ma hoose

dead normal

shipwreck

noah surreal kinda confusion
jist ordinry
marroond

nyi feel like yirra sailir
think yir heids peter pans
n only a wean wid think its excitin
yinno

thi kwik swipe roon thi shelfs

whinyi
wahnti topple aw thi tins
n see thum roll n bounce n burst
n looks n othir faces say

-ah alwiz wahntidti dae that

but you goat ther furst!

more empires

am anartyfarty type me

ma main concern is
talkin ti statues n paintings
asif they wur human beings

ma mates ur arty farty anaw
but they prefer gettin folks
nickers aff

sex
thats whit it aw comes doon ti

thi contention
(after a conversation with Ivan McCammond)

that boundry
that is   the sound uv yir ain voice
thi wan yi wur bornti
might we well be a trap that makes yi fall
inti prejudice

jist coz
sumbdy dizny talk
thi same way you dae
might well make yi think
fuck them
but thats jist snobbery anaw
still

64

touchin

no an object uv art
no sumhn clivir n contempry
jist a few words
ti say thirs nuthin like it

a good kiss n cuddle
your body
ma body   touchin
thats iz good izyi kin get

insecure

yi feel nae sensa self worth
yi feel useless
useless izit   aye

yi feel lonely n misunnirstood
whits ti unnirstawn
ah dont know

ah jist dont know
yir thinkin aw thi time
wake up

fur godsake wake up
none uv that mattirs
dizit? anymer

it dizny mattir anymer
whityi tellin mi
yi remembir this   yi minda that

thi two uv yi
in that wee single bed
aw christ romantic   wintit

a walkin lassoo

thir gawny miss thi bus
aw fuck

shouldny huv steyed fur
wan last pint

so what
am jist nthi park masel

swivvl n spin
lik a walkin lassoo

dancin bravado
winkin starlight

ah tear aff ma claze

leap

nthi
kelvingrove fountain

climb

joyful n wet
ti its jagged

peak

no rememberin
thimorra

through the night air a voice

THROUGH THE NIGHT AIR A VOICE
SPEAKS QUIETLY

huv yi been ti alabama
huv yi goat yir silk pyjamas
yi know it kin get cawld
n thi rats kin make yi waken

gnaw at yir guts
so they dae
gnaw at yir guts
nyir chist n breathins fucked

sleep inside where its warrm
no oot here where its wet
am warnin yi theyll get yi yet
put yi somewhere warrm
n take away yir freedom

THROUGH THE NIGHT AIR A VOICE
you are under arrest
SPEAKS QUIETLY

no kind of haiku ataw

aw right
no long noo
weelbiwellpished nwarrm

*****

SONGS TO DROWN A MILLION SOULS

INTRODUCTION

The verses that follow concern very public and well documented events in the lives of ten artists who made huge contributions to African-American music. Their life stories give an entry point into an exploration of the history and development of American, European and African cultures since the beginning of the slave-trade in the middle 1600s to the present day. The verses are unashamedly didactic and they are genuinely unpolished in the best equivalent of a 'bluesological' style that I -as a white Scottish male- could create. I have chosen these particular ten artists to write about purely from personal taste and they reflect in some part the music I like to listen to. I hope that the language itself also contains some music, and will give people pause for reflection on the kind of world in which we all might one day hope to live. In this sense the verses are idealistic. There is a short essay at the end entitled 'Coming out of Slavery' which elaborates, explains and tries to bring closer to reality the ideas which have informed the writing.

jim ferguson,
Glasgow,
October 6, 2012.

JOE KING OLIVER 1885-1938

born in Apen, Louisiana
in 1885
spent his youth in New Orleans
made the cornet come alive

always optimistic
always on the move
blowin the blues in the streets and bars
his sound was totally new

the largest and the loudest
fire in body and soul
he could make the cornet weep real tears
he could make that gold horn speak

Joe was king of Dixie
Joe was Doctor Jazz

he was the cornet king of New Orleans
they say he took Buddy Bolden's crown
and Joe was king of Chicago too
with his big-blues-dance-band sound

he was the king of wah wah wah
a master on the mute
a towel draped around his neck
to keep the sweat off his suit

Louis Armstrong called him Papa
they played some mean duets
down at the Lincoln Gardens
Joe and Louis were the best

spent his last years as a janitor
because his teeth were bad
trapped in Savannah, Georgia
no longer livin large

where ever there had been emptiness
where ever there was despair
when King Joe Oliver blew that horn
joy jumped through the air

just cleanin in a pool hall now
whistlin the Dippermouth Blues
smilin to himself a while
no longer in the news

hat tipped over his blind left eye
leanin against a wall
this giant mountain of jazz
soundin the last bugle call

in the year of 1938
he sounded his last trumpet call

LOUIS SATCHMO ARMSTRONG 1901-1971

Satchmo, Satchmo
where'd you go
tell me where'd you go
Satchmo

you got out of the orphanage
when you met Papa Joe
an you went on the riverboat
man you could sing an blow

an you went to Chicago
man you could sing an blow
an you went to Europe
man you could sing an blow

an you went to Hollywood
man you could sing an blow

you made the world wonderful
from
the Colored Waifs' Home for Boys
in sultry New Orleans
to
the icy peaks of the Alps
and New York theatre dreams
nothin on earth could hold you back
your heart was much too strong
you play it like you sing it
an you made the world your song
nothin on earth could keep you down
on your breath the folk did rise

in joy and sweet dignity
an smilin pure an high

Satchmo, Satchmo
let's go forward
conquer history
for your sound helps all good folk rise
an to hell with slavery, an to hell with slavery

where ever you are Louis Armstrong
there is no slavery
blow that golden horn my man
blow free   blow free   blow free

HUDDIE LEAD BELLY LEDBETTER 1888-1949

a great cotton pickin country lad
from the rural Louisiana south
the nearest folks lived miles away
from their little farm house
Hugh-Dee was as strong as an ox
could pick the cotton real fast
but his real love was music an song
barrelhouse, an havin a blast

he was master songster
with a massive repertoire
train songs, work songs, prison songs
god, drink an drug songs too
love songs for feelin lonesome
an love songs for oohh hoo hoo
songs of slavery an segregation
songs of poverty an hard life

he knew the prison from inside
work-farm an chain-gang too
but always he was collectin songs
an storing them in his mind
so when they came from the Congress Library
they can't believe what they find
a man with so many songs in hand
they thought to record them down

an even when he was some kinda legend
preferred the red lights of Dallas town
they say he carried and a knife an a gun
was a hard man to be around
but him an Blind Lemon Jefferson

played many a great duet
deep down there in Dallas
that folk could never forget

on the low notes he played hard
strummin his guitar
to sound like a piano
playin 12 bar bass note blues
and gently pickin the high notes
or slidin sweetly up n down
when you hear him play n sing
you know it only he that got that sound
 - it only he that got that sound

BESSIE SMITH 1894-1937

big of heart
big of voice
big like a statue
immense as an ocean
big songs to drown a million souls

Bessie raise you up
an Bessie take you down

makin men weep in late night bars
an cry beneath the hot day sun —
where is mama, my mama's gone
an my daddy is crazy on wine -
where's mama, my mama's gone
an my daddy's crazy on wine -
feel juss like a poor little orphan
although am thirty nine

Bessie take you down
an Bessie she raise you up

she got the Jail House Blues
she got the St Louis Blues
she got the Downhearted Blues
she got the Empty Bed Blues
she got the Thinkin Blues
she got them Mean Old Bedbug Blues
she got the Rockin Chair Blues
she got the Need Money Blues

she's the Empress of the Blues

born in Chattanooga, Tennessee
in1894
she could sing before she could walk
got the blues in her DNA

by the age of 14
she sounded so good
Ma Rainey thought to take her on tour
raw an bold she didn't like cold
an she didn't like singin in tents

in 1923
things all goin her way
she sold over 2 million records
from the north to the south
she filled every house
the greatest woman to ever sing the blues

loved by women an men
and by folk white an black
she never needed a mic
she was true to her soul
but didn't think twice
bout drinkin down a half-pint of gin

these were the times she lived in
these were the times she lived in
times that keep on changing
so you don't know where to begin

she knew what it was to go hungry
she knew what poverty meant
then when she made all that money
she gave it away an she spent

an Bessie was rough an ready
an Bessie was meek as a lamb
an when in that car she was ridin
it crashed into a van
an though they pulled her out alive
that's when her real troubles began
that's when her real troubles began

the hospital said 'no admission'
they did not want any blacks
by the time she got to the next place
she was never comin back

by the time she got to the next hospital
she was dead
she was never comin back

LEON 'BIX' BEIDERBECK 1903-1931

roarin trumpet
cornet smooth an sweet
mellow piano
strollin through the mist of life
with a drink in his hand
an never too far from delirium tremens
Bix was a strange jazz fish

middle-class and white
a german-american
somehow born to a blue kind of boogie
at Davenport, Iowa, in the year of 1903.

sittin waitin for riverboats
on the Mississippi banks
to hear music of the south
the young Bix would climb aboard and jam
he was a self-taught trumpeter
with a style all of his own
free an fast an beautiful
such a pure an mellow tone

he made young folk happy
he made them bop all night
to drink and see them dancing
that was his delight
jazz was his music of choice
the blues they gave him hope
an when he heard Bessie Smith
he asked her never to stop

sometimes he was forgetful
one day he forgot what to play

his nerves were frayed an fretful
then in a hospital he lay
he tried to work on recovery
but his teeth didn't have enough strength
so he sat in a room in Queens
played piano with slow elegance

an Bix he had lived fast
an Bix he did die young
a romantic-unromantic legend
like those rock stars yet to come

THOMAS FATS WALLER 1904-1943

Fats was the son of preacher
he went against the grain
his father didn't like it
but he went forward just the same
at the Lincoln Theatre, Harlem
he played the organ there
a big and brash 14 year old
with a talent that was rare

always up for a drink an a smoke
always crackin crazy jokes
Fats recorded the reefer song
just to have a laugh at the cops
he played a mighty boogie piano
wrote over 400 songs
his was the best version of Tea for Two
ever to come along
an when he says,
You're Socks Don't Match,
you can bet it's gonna be true
you can bet it's gonna be true

with irony, humour an mischief
he played the music of the devil
an when Al Capone held a gun to his head
he smiled an kept on playin
Fats he didn't see nothin,
didn't hear what the gangsters were saying
an at that gangster party
he played three nights and days
an when he finally left there

he was drunk an tired an rich
but most of all he was glad
to be lyin in no ditch,
yupp, most of all he was glad
he wasn't in no ditch

somehow he caught pneumonia
an died aged thirty nine
yet out of the pain of his people
came this music that sounded so fine
he wrote his London Symphony
an his music was so mighty fine

BILLIE LADY HOLIDAY 1915-1959

a lost leaf
a little girl

a tree
with strong yet slender branches

but
always the axes

moving towards you

*

bereft humanity
bleeding New York cunts

streamers and ticker-tape
beautifully flying

*

nothing from
heaven

except your voice

who knows why
there's no sweet charity

82

*

numb your heart
sing away

weep and say

*strange fruit
hanging
from the poplar tree*[1]

PAUL LEROY ROBESON 1898-1976
*'The artist must take sides. He must elect to fight for
freedom or slavery.
I have made my choice. I had no alternative.'*

your mother strangely devoured by flames,
accidentally, in the house
where she'd given you birth, a memory that
remained forever locked-up in your six-year-old
head

twas then your father, a breaker of bread,
took the work of raising you up,
motherless siblings,
in a parish church at Witherspoon Street

with an all black congregation
but the decisions all made by Princeton whites,
lessons in injustice learned,
an inscrutable knowledge of right

---

[1] Originally a poem by Abel Meeropol.

83

and wrong, was formed early in your mind,
your father was, like,
Gil Scott Heron & Brian Jackson & Langston
Hughes, a student at Lincoln College

while that other college at Princeton
long refused to let blacks in,
maybe old Witherspoon turned in his grave
or maybe he didn't bother

when his fine ivy school at Princeton
refused entry for your brother
and your father lost his pastor's job
for protesting a little too much —

he forced Woodrow Wilson to declare
that Princeton did not accept 'colored',
those guardians of democracy, with
Scottish Presbyterian traditions

could not let a black man
darken their sanctified halls —
equality would not shine therein
their dignity was small —

and long is the road to freedom
and deep is the river of hate
but we all shall overcome
be made welcome at the gate —

Paul was a first-rate student
won a scholarship to Rutger's school
there he excelled as an athlete
as an orator and singer too

84

but his journey was tough and complex
he followed a difficult track
they changed their own rules just to thwart him
and he still knocked them onto their backs

a proud and thoughtful giant
he went to Columbia to study law
but after graduation
all he found before him was walls

so he went to work in theatre
where he sung and took acting parts
on stage he was a colossus
part of the Harlem Renaissance in arts

he led in plays by Eugene O'Neill
and soon was acting in movies
but life would take on new zeal
when he met with Spanish Revolutionaries

he became a political artist
a man with a cause and a vision
a world free from bigotry and oppression
was now his eternal mission

and for this he paid very dearly
the historians they airbrushed him out
they took away his passport
but he did not turnabout

race riots dogged him severely
especially at Peeksgill, New York,
violence from fascists and haters
was viewed by the Police as fair sport

but Robeson was unbowed
his dignity it was immense
he packed as much into one life-time
as most could make out of ten

his voice carried all round the planet
to Scotland, England, Ireland and Wales
so profoundly deep, making folks weep
in Paris and Moscow and Brussels

he sang *The Ballad of Joe Hill*
and he sang *Ole Man River* too,
songs that were anthems for many
in a voice that rang out clear and true

there aint no hammer that rings like mine —

to McCarthy's Red Scare Committee he stated:
*'my father was a slave, and my people died to build
this country,
and I am going to stay here, and have a part of it
just like you.
And no Fascist-minded people will drive me from
it. Is that clear?'*[2]

---

[2] Robeson, Paul Leroy, Testimony of Paul Robeson before the
House Committee on Un-American Activities, June 12, 1956.

but the FBI and CIA made Paul Robeson almost
disappear, never the less his story survives
and his singing voice brings us nearer
—to a sense of dignity and striving

—to an end to the horrors of lynching
—to an end to the laws of Jim Crow -
Paul Robeson's voice takes us closer
—to a world of justice and hope

Paul Robeson's life and struggle
bring us
closer
—to a world of justice and hope

CHARLIE BIRD PARKER 1920-1955

'I always thought that music should be clean ...
Something that was beautiful.'

blow that alto sax Bird
play in double quick time
bring on the birth of bebop
transform the musical rules
be big an brash an lucid
be mellow like honey in tea
don't grow up too fast young man
your storms won't let you be

you came out of Kansas City
bright, new and fiery blue
Art Tatum was your inspiration
when washin dishes was what you do
an you took his piano style
applied it to the alto sax
to make a brand new sound
that knocked folks on their back

you were jamming with Chet Baker
Miles Davis was your friend
Buddy Rich kept beat for you
with Dizzy you was groovin high
Lester Young an Coleman Hawkins
Ella Fitzgerald too
live at Carnegie Hall in September 1949
an amazing *Embraceable* time

sittin back with a cigarette
an a little glass of wine
or practicing 15 hours day

to get those notes sublime
tradin blues with Buster Smith
before it was time to bob, bebop
come flyin out of the traps
racing like a train, tearin up the tracks

say goodbye to sanity
in good old LA town
set your bed on fire
an have a long lie down
up there on the bandstand
not a worry or a care
or stayin in the hospital
until your head was clear

they took your cabaret card
an would not let you work —
then you swallowed iodine
your child not too long dead —
when the FBI they hounded you
Europe was where you fled —
takes a strong man to live with that
takes all the strength of the old

ancestors who came before us
an all those yet to come
all who love music an freedom
who blow an strike an drum
bring on your huge appetite for life
bring on the orchestra bold
take off your shoes an socks
come in out of the cold

take the weight off your feet
let your body breathe
go to sleep sweet Yardbird
fly away into dreams
float into death young Charlie
float n fly   float n fly   float n fly
fly away Bird
fly away

                                fly away

        fly away

                                        Bird

                fly away

                                        Bird . Bird

                                        fly

        away

GIL SCOTT-HERON 1949-2011

we aint yet seen a revolution
an there aint no end of pain
but folks continue fightin just the same

Gil's father played for Celtic
the Black Arrow was his name
he came from old Jamaica
and soccer was his game

Gil was born on April fool's day in 1949
at Chicago, Illinois,
his mother she sang opera
before he moved to Tennessee

he was brought up there in Jackson
by his grandmother Lillie
she was a forthright woman
who believed in education an the NAACP

she read the *Chicago Defender*
an the books of Langston Hughes
knew the difference between truth an lies
helped Gil form his views

Lillie died when Gil was 13
an he moved up to the Bronx
stayed there with his mother
in the big city of New York

already the blues had caught him
jazz an latin rhythms too
the poetry within his soul
would soon be shinin through

a bright an able student
he was never no dumb fuck
yet fate has a way of trapping us all
into our own kind of luck

...

*

a temporary interruption
to the bare statement of events —

you know you have to say something
don't worry bout the form
or be too obsessed with technique
it's only really democracy when everyone can speak
don't worry bout your tone, don't worry bout the
sound
real artistry and freedom is getting things done and
down -
some critics will try to fuck you
by saying the thing is too *this* or too *that*
but who the hell really cares
and where the hell is their art

these arbiters of taste
they're just standing on the sidelines
not makin their own way
just talkin bout other peoples' work
an pocketing the weekly pay -
so put your poems on the table
put your light up on the screen
and let us hear what you gotta say
if you wanna be a clean human being
let us hear your voice
let us see your vision —
send the critics back under their rocks
to send out their derision —

let's fool around folks
let's fool around

take it down   *take it down*   it's swing time now
take it down

shot him in the head, shot him in
the head, shot him in the head

shot me too --- smoking crack cocaine

sweetly deranged, idiot child, on crack cocaine

boy, boy, boy, swing that hammer
boy, boy, boy, swing that hammer
before the sun goes down
boy, boy, boy, swing that hammer
—with the devil we're all goin down

■ message received ? —

93

*

...

tryin to live through difficult times
an strugglin with addiction
he retained his integrity
an wrote some very fine fiction

some cultures can enslave you
certain rules can make you insane
injustice it can wear you down
permanently damage your brain

poet, novelist and singer
he remained very close to his roots
Gil had that great empathy
lets you walk in other folks' boots

it's a poetry of commitment
a sound that comes from the street
songs of love and revolution
with a bluesological beat

that was the style of Gil
always a straight talkin dude —
he didn't sit on no fence
even when it did him no good

gotta keep becoming human
try to mend them broken hearts
with respect for all men n women
an a dedication to art

in late years he released *i'm new here*
deep an emotionally stark
naked dreams from broken homes
with the hardest an softest of hearts

lord, we aint seen no revolution
an there aint no end of pain
but folks continue fightin just the same
lord, folks continue fightin just the same

COMING OUT OF SLAVERY

There is a direct line from slavery to the blues. Those who in the past believed, and in the present believe slavery a good idea might congratulate themselves on one thing. Out of the slavery of African-Americans came a unique chain of musical movements that has thrilled, delighted and made life more bearable for millions of people on the planet. Music that is perhaps the most tangible 'silver lining' to have come out of the barbarism that took place over the three hundred years or so when Africans were tricked, bribed or kidnapped and transported in the most horrific of conditions to the Americas and the Caribbean. 'Of the 35 to 40 million involved in the trade to the Americas ... an estimated 15 million survived the journey'.[3] This statistic reveals the population of Scotland over the 300 year period being wiped out on around 24 occasions. The slave-trade was genocide in slow-motion. Or, if it had happened in an instant, it would entail the wiping out of 4 or 5 present day Scotlands.

The fact that those who survived the horrors of transportation then went on to live lives so abhorrent to the condition of being a human being further adds to the overall misery that many millions of black people and others have endured over an unbelievably long period. A period that encompasses the Scottish Enlightenment, the French Revolution and other moments in history where folk tried to put an end to servitude, mindless royalism, slavery and indentured labour. In fact during that period when many so-called civilised cultural and humanitarian values were being thought through there always seemed to

---

[3] Oakley, Giles, *The Devil's Music: a history of the blues*, Da Capo, 1997, p.14.

be certain groups of people who were exceptions: people who were somehow not human or did not qualify for the same treatment in terms of human rights and justice as those who were making the laws.

The entire capital base and economic prosperity of the Southern US states were based upon the labour of slaves and black people. The ports of Bristol and Liverpool in the UK also thrived on the backs of black slaves and poor white working people. Very little of the wealth produced by black slaves ever found its way back to them, nor did it find its way into the hands of poor whites. Poor whites remained and remain poor, and in the City of Glasgow where I am sitting writing this piece now (in 2012) the levels of poverty are startlingly high, as are all the associated ills of poverty; mental health problems, physical health problems, drug & alcohol addiction and so on. Such is the structure of the economy here that there are never sufficient jobs to go round. Yet politicians of all hues and none seek to blame the fact of the existence of their impoverished countrymen and women on some kind of shiftlessness, and individual irresponsibility. This kind of exercise has been going on since the earliest beginnings of the Industrial Revolution, during which time ruling elites have almost always blamed the poor for their poverty. That this idea is now allied with the free-market and socially conservative attitudes to constitute a more or less worldwide ideology, is as worrying as the ignoble treatment of Africans and African-Americans. Rarely has a ruling elite considered the creation, re-creation and perpetuation of poverty as having anything to do with its own policies and actions.

What we now have is a global system of wage slavery at best, and at worst forced labour and slavery. It appears to be 'controlled' by the IMF/World Bank, the private banks, private global corporations and by the oil and other

97

strategic interests of governments. All of whom are guilty of forms of imperialism and robbery. That brazen robbery is dressed up and sold as the spread of democracy, law and civilisation is the saddest of human ironies.

Those who have been most thoroughly robbed -where ever they happen to be- are most easily blamed for their own plight. It is through their own individual will that they have made themselves poor. The absurd stupidity of this line of argument is plain: it is out of a deep understanding of such absurdity that blues music and other forms of cultural resistance to tyranny evolve. It is well illustrated in the treatment of so-called 'runaway' slaves, who were beaten severely only to run away again be re-captured and beaten again. The situation is impossible from the point of view of the slave; slaves are criminals for asserting their right to a free human life. And yet they continue to strive for freedom regardless of the beatings and criminalisation, but it appears to those in control that the slave wants to be punished and beaten. The slave is at fault! Why else keep running away?

By the 1890s musical forms had coalesced around Mississippi and adjoining states that were highly specific to African-Americans. Although slavery had been outlawed in 1865 it was quickly replaced by a system of segregation laws in the South and ghettoisation in the Northern USA, both required and still require an enormous struggle of spirit and commitment to overcome. Yet, with this greater but still limited freedom and in spite of systematic economic discrimination a great musical movement came to the attention of millions. It is music that has its roots in the experience of the African-American slave and whether we wish to call it blues, barrelhouse, boogie-woogie, rag-time, jazz, bebob, cool, soul or hip-hop is not the point. 'So spirituals and field hollers are connected to the blues, the blues to bebop, jazz and soul'.[4] All of it is connected to the African-American slave experience and the struggles of these people to overcome the hardships they encountered during hundreds of years of oppression. Perhaps this is why the blues and jazz fly so freely into improvisation, call and response, dance and rhythmic chant; they literally throw off oppression in the moment of performance.

It is a musical movement that has produced artists of great genius. Indeed there are blues and jazz compositions that are easily the equal of European classics composed by Bach, Beethoven and Stravinsky. Never the less there are countless millions of people who have carried this music of freedom in their hearts and minds and passed it on largely unnoticed through generations, as well as across geographical and cultural borders. Musical expression is one form of cultural freedom. It was one of the few forms of African expression not completely wiped out on the cotton-plantation or by the chain-gang.

In the lives of the women and men I have written some verses about here, there resides part of the struggle for genuine human freedom and expression. And if readers who live in Scotland now wish to continue the struggle against wage slavery and cultural slavery it can partly be done at the ballot box in 2014 by voting for Scottish independence. So, at last, after more than 300 years, Scottish culture too, might breathe a little more freely.

---

[4] Turkel, Studs, *Giants of Jazz*, New York, 2002, pp. 170-171

BRAIN FEVER

having covered a lot of ground
poor auld martin eden drowned

a vast systemic tragedy, the end

angelic and devilish

Angelic   Devilish
      and!
hobbling yet flying
          down the street
into town
     with
too many thoughts
       of the gunshot
that pierced Mayakovsky's

Guts   Heart
in the clouds with moon-faced Lily

upon whom
         his love-boat crashed
—smashed
—crushed
by
    'poetry's
         toil-worn hands'
no cloud in his trousers

nothing
     to keep him
standing

       Not
in the sky or the earth
     beneath
nor way down below yonder
     where the fiends all creep

101

—He crawled and he soared,
so ultimately floated

Devilish   Angelic
        and!

into that unnameable

        town.

bus x bus = bus

this boy don't take no subway
this boy don't take no train
he only got the sus for the bus into town
and aint got the eyes of the sane

if only he could raise an arm
   twould be thus he could hail a cab
      instead he leans his body, too relaxed,
         on the bus-shelter's thick glass pane

stupid smile bolted on his lips
he's a drunk or a junkie or mad
cause nobody smiles like that
              —all irrational and blinking
he can see other folk wonder
what the fuck he is thinking
cause to smile like that he must
be a drunk or a junkie or mad
or possibly plain old bad

he puts the fear in the air
pours paranoia into the heart

as wee boys in go-carts
scoot by and scream
but they move in slow-motion
all blood-red and seem

like they're heading for a crash
like they're heading for death

for tragedy unbound, and unbidden
  like a lightning bolt from heaven
    but the boys all laugh and disappear off
      round a corner as

the queue starts to move
our man ambles in
to a smooth seat groove
and they're off

doors slide shut
doors slide shut

'screw the nut,' he thinks
  keeps the smile bolted on
    as a song starts to issue
      from his mad, alcoholic, junkie lips:

this boy don't take no subway
this boy don't take no train
he only got the sus for the first omnibus
and he aint got the eyes of the sane

the crowd

step down into the city crowd
organised chaos, of course,
        random yet ordered
all juxtapositions
and oxymoronic

hard-shelled crabs
        soft-skinned humans
insects scuttling
        a dignified sea of strollers

what call to arms!
  charity girls raising funds
   in bright yellow and orange
    all breasts and teeth
     to unhinge the wallets

he looks downward
into the pavement crack dreams
of the footfalls of previous travellers
long since buried by cirrhosis

        a woman is heart-attack dead
on the red of George Square
while the medics fumble with blankets

cover and carry the body
on a cold aluminium stretcher

that's why they need the blankets
so important to cover the head

so important to keep the dead soft
so important to be soft in the hard-shelled city
to keep your humanity warm

this crowd is crazy
capable of anything — riot
revolution and looting
but everyone here is too busy shopping

it is peacefully organised chaos
as policemen lurk in corners with guns
alas

first first person

i mean (one is)

well

i mean

i mean well

in at the bar
3 pints quick

rapid

baramaid's name
is lianne

little badge
says so

mental note
of that

chit chat
then out

i mean
a daunder out

for air
and nicotine

then back
in at the bar

3 pints quick
rapid lianne

means well
too

chit chat
most unfortunate

eye injury
cut and black

while falling
off the bus

you'd better be more careful, says lianne,
what did you're missus say? if

my man came home like that
he'd know all about it.

i do know all about, says i,
it's not like it's quantum physics

simple newtonian mechanics
suffice to describe the

falling
motion.

that's not what i mean, she says.
i know what she means

she means well —
3rd pint down

time
to take a walk

well
round

i mean well
(one is)

square within the square

four park benches
shuvved onto the grass —
organised into a square
          by enterprising afternoon amblers

asylum seeking suncatchers
take their chance to relax
in the abnormal warmth
of this springing day

light ricochets from his
hunter thomson hat
          which flattens his
          malcolm mclaren hair

keeps the stray thoughts
from straying anywhere
they can do any damage —
keeps them safely locked away

and over he strolls joining
park bench relaxers
          all very mellow —
          earth is green and yellow

he electrically thinks
as he parks his arse down:

what brings you to this godforsaken town?
electricity, the absence of torture,
a boat, a plane, an unstoppable train
-with lenin inside and superman's brain

on an accurate scale, as if
its weight corresponds to its gigantic thoughts!-
food, something that makes you feel good, yeah,
it's a remarkable day for this city,

just having a drink and a think,
hence the hat, it's a day
to walk freely, without fear or favour —
savour the planet, the wee people on it

what do you think of the bonnet?
the bunnet, the flat cap and skip
        they all keep different thoughts
        locked in the skull, yet others escape

make it away — out into the world
to do all sorts of cultural tumbles and twirls —
march down 10th avenue, or through red
square, or into the sadness of european history

that tangles in your hair
  and african history,
    tangles in your hair
    and indian history,
      tangles in your hair
      and chinese history,
        tangles in your hair
        and aboriginal history,
          tangles in your hair
          and the history of history,
            tangles in your hair
but this small story of
sitting back smoking in the springtime sun
lingers with us,
          — romantic, hard-won

our fragile friends
our precious lovers
the best we have seen,
all human, some here, some gone

onward

walk on through the town
say hello here and there
he gives a woman the fear
by smiling too close to her face

it's rare for her to be out of her car
she thinks that public spaces are
meant to afford her privacy
but everywhere she sees threats —

chance upon chance -that's what you take
when you dare to go out —
why cameras and policemen and nosey bastards
are always lurking about

the words 'civil liberty'
stuck in the throat of
a lead-boxed corpse
buried 12 foot down

he smiles at the pelican crossing
waits until it starts talking
then crosses with the sound
does a wee dance around with the beeps

idiot thinkings

under the
oppressive phallus
of the tolbooth

many pubs
nestle together —

irony
upon
irony

this is
celtic
irish
territory

traditionally
place of executions
hangings and taxes
primal anti-freedoms

designed to
let us be free
apparently
time to
pop in
and drink

sing and dance
and squeeze
a wee tear
in the foggy dew

*

then into
a new
transeuropean
café

for coffee
strong
coffee

then into
an auld
artists
pub

for coffee
strong
coffee

*

finding
a hungarian
man
named jan
quite
happy go lucky
off they go
for a cabaret

excitement
poets
musical
chants

shouting
and
having
a rant
is totally
unacceptable

now
out on the street
god knows
why or how
but hugely
disappointed
after the
young man
with the
security
ear-piece
had taken
hold of
his arm
and forced
him through
the exit

no cabaret
for him
tonight
no doubt
even after
the

coffees
strong
coffees

he was
still pretty
high
with the
booze

he guessed
there were
new rules
for parties
these days

but he hadn't
heard that
on the news

though he'd heard
many other
fear-filling
truths

second first person

aye,
she says i wisny that bad

disny
fuckin mattir but

still
the guilt

always
the guilt

what kind of world?
aye

always
have to ask questions

always
push towards the mirage

die
of thirst

cause yi took a wrong turn
— mistakes

are allowed
but

one must

go home

and sleep them off

go home
and sleep them off

sit on the settee
even daytime tv

stoo intense
fuck me

jewellery and electrical goods preferred

the spirit of jim morrison
not totally extinct

he celebrated
the rise of the new pawn-shop

by taking
in his horse and asking for a ticket

perfectly

o
f
cours
e,

as
the
old
sayi
ng
goes
:

there's a perfectly *good parallel universe next door*

thinks he'll try in there
for a drink and a wee bit banter

maybe a tequila
with salt and lime

fires it over
into the belly

dances round his hat
on one leg

trippy face
falling onto the floor

his face is tripping him
his face is tripping him

is it time yet for a greet?

time yet for tears?

see the state of that
        mexican hat-dance — tears and snotters
                fly through the air

two legged dancing
        is safer — hit them with your rhythm stick

coz it's *sex n drugs n rock n roll*
        and — of course,

it's none of the above
        it's afternoon tea and scones

it's olives and oatcakes
        and a selection of the finest cheeses

it's a perfectly formed world
land   —   sea   —   river   —   and sky

pillow talk

who ever used this pillow before
        had had some very weird thoughts

suddenly they crept down his follicles,
        somehow got through his skull and sneaked

right into his dreamtime brain
        some woman singing in the background

got the fever!
ah got the fever!

meanwhile, a dude in the corner was saying:
 why don't you invade that part of the world,

 why don't you invade the part of world
 formerly known as palestine but now called

 the state of Israel? —
i'm a pacifist, he muttered,

woke with a start and a splutter —
 sat on the edge of his bed and pondered

it was all too fucking much...
 the pillows of thought control

were on the march!
 he'd never seen the likes

not since the coal miners
 went on strike

back in
 1984

— a bad year that

the grapes produced
 no drinkable wines

it was all too fucking hard to swallow...

third first person

having breakfasted
on humble porridge

i took my fevered brain
to
     alcoholics anonymous
       grumpy fuckers anonymous
        narcotics anonymous
         pillows anonymous
          gamblers anonymous
           violent-heids anonymous
            david bowies anonymous
             post-modernists anonymous
            absurdists anonymous —

always anonymous
i checked myself into *the priory*

put the plug in the bath
buried myself in the water
breathed it in and drowned

just like

     poor auld martin eden drowned
     having covered a lot of ground

     a vast systemic tragedy, the end
     — then started all over again

121

TWENTY ITEMS ON THE NATURE OF WIND

1

Just a particularly
usual morning,
wake up
fart

go to the bathroom.
Sit down to write
some usual things

and just be particularly
struck on a usual morning
with the word
fart.

Is it poetic enough
that kind of thing.
That particularly usual word
fart.

2

Content and form,
what can I say?

I don't know the answer
to what comes first,

questions or answers.

But, then there must be
somekind of meaning.

Avoid bad puns.
That's what I've been told.

Form and content
and false dichotomies

forever.

3

It's just being alive.
Being gentle, being cruel, trying
to keep going and not do too much
damage.

Who are those who would trespass
against us.

Is it a question of class.
Haircuts.
Styles of dress.
Or merely the vocal chords?
The right to exploit, even
the thoughts in your head.

4

It's a different approach in a way
Sounds,
        concretes,
                performances.

But, maybe it isn't different.
All just process.

Best and worst.
Science and laws.

Ideas and history.
Language and ideology.
Language.

5

If some folk still want to use
iambic pentameter,

that's fine.

6

If some folk don't want to use
any pentameter, iambic or otherwise

that's fine.

7

If somebody wants to play the sound
of a fart through a tape recorder.

Fine.

That's very liberal. Maybe that's not fine.

That's fine!

8

Having sat at the table for some time
on a cold January morning.

It makes sense to
go over to the gas fire for a heat.

That's fine too.
As long as you can pay the bills.

9

Having introduced economics!/one is/
tempted to talk about the "economy of language".

10

Having introduced economics,/one is/
tempted to talk about the economics of accent

the economics of accent and colour
the economics of accent and colour, race
and freedom of movement
the economics of accent and colour, race
and freedom of movement and what is meant by
"Fortress Europe"?

11

One is tempted to talk about politics.

12

One is tempted to talk about religion.

126

13

One is not tempted to talk about these
things at all, as they aren't supposed
to be mentioned in pubs, polite company,
or in the poetry that emanates from
Oxford or Cambridge.
Though in the case of the last two, it
is allowed if done with delicacy.

14

I don't like all this poetry
which takes as its subject matter
the writing of poetry.

15

The opposite of 14.

16

Can numbers have opposites?
Negative.

17

This is absurd!

18

"This is absurd",
is a statement
only to be used by
the upper middle-classes
and super-rich
when referring to
existential angst.

19

Existential angst, is often experienced
by the lower orders when they fart
in delicate company or that of their superiors.
Of course, they have no conception of what
existential angst is, so spend half their lives
walking about in a state of deep *alienation.*

19 and a hauf

They don't know what *alienation* means either.

20

It's back to the same old questions,
from Aristotle to the Romantics.
Through classicism, neo-classicism,
all kinds of movements, aesthetic values,
and poetic creeds.

It's just so much better to wake up
have a good fart and write,
if that's how you feel.

A Simple Guide to the Present Ideology

greed: the carrot

poverty: the stick

prejudice: the lubricant

mendacity: the insurance

fear: the censor

all things imprisoned
inside one market
slapped and punched
by the crazy coercion
of some 'hidden hand'

it's
- a market for money
- a market for ideas
- a market for humans
- a market for murder
- a market for space
- a market for air
- a market for every
thing

an unwritten law

TRAVELS IN A DRIFTING LIVING ROOM
ON SAUCHIEHALL STREET, GLASGOW

1

high wind, rain
rumbling traffic
the roar of the bus
with people going places

moving across the city,
fitting into slots;
all sense of belonging rooted
firmly in the minds buoyancy

trees sway and their tops
might fly away
but always they hold firm
against the wind

2

this is not a day
for tea at the ritz
or going to the races
for cosy drinks of whisky and beer

it is a domestic scene;
staying in, rooted, here,
ironing shirts for future wear
keeping appearances, taking care

this is not a day
for mild contemplation
of literary plans, or action
but a day, as often, for considering

the pseudo-liberals,
who will not spare the weight
of their police and military
to keep power in their hands

3

on discovering the fact that
i am the owner of certain foodstuffs
i feel a bit surprised at this surplus of wealth
enough food for seven days and ten until the giro?

answers on a milk coupon!
available from the department of social security,
should you have difficulty obtaining such a coupon
a postcard will suffice!

4

crawling across the hall carpet
towards the kitchen
is quite a journey, maybe
about ten yards in total

it's not so far
even after two days without food;
then how to reach the light switch
when you're on your knees?

answers on a postcard please!

5

having stared at trees and rain,
and other elements, that communing
with nature through the window,
listening to the city's sounds;

buses, cats, pigeons, rats,
cars, voices, sirens, bats,
seagulls, rain again, and howling wind
the temptation is to forget

about the city's underbelly,
the secret deals and insurance fires
addicts, beggars, and burnt out bodies,
things falling from the back of lorries,

and the greasing of elected palms;
what is the estimated rat population of glasgow?
answers on a district council rent rebate form,
you may exclude the city chambers from your answer!

squeak, squeak, squeak,

6

these days much attention is paid
to tidying the city by uprooting trees,
of course
this does not trouble the urban proletariat

only the middle classes are interested in trees
or enjoy the fact that trees exist
trees are not even trade union members
and have scabbed on many disputes

real bastards those trees,
chop them down and improve the city;
nothing beats a good healthy motorway,
is carbon monoxide a very good gas?

answers on a recycled postcard please!

7

the city planners
are a mighty interesting bunch,
especially the labour members
of the planning committee

they are the stuff poetry is made of,
to be with them is to experience the poetry
of good administration and all-above-board
dealings;
is this not true?

don't bother with an answer!

8

this country
a thistle, a ruin,
crumpled and thwarted
by rose and thorn

this place of sweat,
grime and swearing,
shouting, alcohol
and drugs, and the pride

of serving colonial masters
of ravaging the world
as we are ravaged, and the shame
of our forebears and contemporaries

taking the royal shilling

9

a cup of tea
is a great tonic
especially
if it's scottish blend

but as good internationalists
we understand the meaning
of the tea pot and the darkness
squirrelled within the spout;

where a plantation worker
is shouting in muffled tones
about a banana republic
and one-crop dependency

the values of decency and
fair play; the rules
that destroyed
the worker's words

language
ripped from the throat
butchered
in the name of christ

10

coal could well be wonderful
texture black and moody;
the digging of it dangerous
the geology quite treacherous

but this is no treachery
when compared to the british government
who are stitching a deal
for their wealthy friends

while making us pay
their nuclear tax;
they will scrap forty thousand jobs
they will sell us all

make private all of public life;
money is king
people are rubbish;
people are not worth mentioning?

answers on a postcard please!

11

the good sweet government
is keen to upset *citizens*
in the name of progress;
we live as happy and free **subjects**

of her majesty,
on this little island
of liberty and tolerance;
aren't you proud to be a british subject?

answers on a postcard please!

12

where to go in the world?
more difficult than it may seem;
inside Fortress Europe
democracy means money

freedom means a large amount;
to cross a border
is tolerable when profitable;
who would be a refugee?

answers on a postcard please!

13

to go to the post office
means going outside;
is it safe?

posting postcards
can be
precarious;

when feeling
fully at home
in the drifting

living room
of time; where
even in its solidity,

you can never
breathe the same oxygen
twice!

answers, care of heraclitus,
kingdom of the dead,
beyond the high wind and rumbling traffic.

going forwards backwards

must be
a lifetime
since the summer

        before the winter years
        set in
        so granite hard
        and cold

when water tasted so much sweeter
on my tongue and into my system
so much easier to catch than now
somehow, in the cells of a soul
baptism from within and such
a consoling flavour, taste, such
a taste at the back of my throat
so clean and free to breathe, to swallow
to swim, to float at night right through
the liquid rhythm of dreams
and wake in the morning early
ready for the day to flow, to flow
and rush into it, waving, waving back
to when water tasted so much sweeter

must be a lifetime since summer
forget what it was like to be
walking out on the killoch glen
with a girl named janet
through long warm days
relaxed yet somehow definite
there would always be somewhere to go
before the cold set in with janet
dressed in her summer dress
looking like the girl forever to smile
and pass away the days so simply
relaxed and far too sure
that things would turn out fine
before they ever tasted bitter

the hot water's run out on me
and this bath is cold
this ice-cube of a bathroom
is no good, no use to me now
with the weather so cold
and flu creeping under my skin
somewhere in the future
there will be warmer waters
brand new summers to walk
again in the killoch glen
look at old names
carved out on trees
if those trees
still stand

learning to sleep with the t.v. on
is one sure sign of too much booze
taken over too short a time
but far too soon years swim away
and when you try to catch them
there's too much weight
too much rough water
to pull your way through,
way too many rapids and falls
what can you do but keep pulling
keep putting the past behind and
moving on as best you can
learn once more to go to sleep
with the t.v. turned off

wandered round my brother's kitchen
searching for a cork-screw
which was hiding when i found
myself thinking of all the times
my brother and i had drank
ourselfs insanely drunk and
in our maudlin state remember
what our father's face
was like when he was happy
but it was too hard for us
not to remember his dark temper
his heavy adult hands
pushing us aside with little understanding
but somehow love

met a woman who kept a cat
and was good company
for a year or two
before my hopeless head
became too much for her to bear
and she ended it
all the women i ever met
who kept cats were special
different from the others who
of course, were fine but didn't last
as long in that place and time
where love stays sentimental
and lives on memory
with a fiery bitter taste

in search of something to wear in bed
a winter woollen maybe for peace
in your sleep you hope it's safe
and warm and you won't die there
frozen and blue
it doesn't matter how many layers
you wrap around to keep out the dark
it's never safe enough to drift
into dreaming without worry
why worry, why not worry,
when the search is taking far too long
and winter woollens are hard to find
worry more, for nothing is ever guaranteed-
where is the morning which never arrives?

lucky to have a bed now
lucky to live where you'll be fed
lucky really that life isn't fair

for if it was what would you say
when tin-plated sarcasm falls away
lucky really lucky to live

with a story to tell of occasional hell
with a story to tell that's halfway happy
lucky really lucky to know happiness now

and again

these words do not know this paper
just fallen here, shot down
in lines compelled to fall
somewhere outside this self
and break the falling future
falling future after falling future
falling faster and breaking outside
brightness, everything's dark
too dark, too dark to fix
an eye upon
an eye to fix with
an eye to see outside
beyond these words
this paper doesn't know

Sorley MacLean is sleeping
the sleep of islands and mountains

his voice sings on the air
and carries round europe

with the certainty of chaos
through this century's turbulence

and when mid-way we had things bad
and worse than bad, the voice of the Gael

carried far around the globe
beyond the reach of oppressors

hogmanay again, another year gone
or muddled through, mad bad and mixed up
raise our whisky's to the sky in hope
and cheer and smile through stony faces
kissing lips and shaking hands and shaking
lips and kissing hands, all's for the best
for aw the best of our tomorrows
and our yesteryears now resting
on our beds of stone and waiting
to walk into our destiny

where's the worry in your eyes come frae
don't know, dunno
want tae tell mi
mind of that song
listen with your eyes
lissnwiyur eyes!
Stupid eh , ih stewpit
awright
alright
maybe i shouldny have asked
shoodnyuv said, says whit ah wizthinkin
mibby eh laybir ullno win
ah widny wurry but
wouldn't worry at all
hoose ih commins
house of commons
house uv cards
n every wan markt
alright
awright
stoap naggin
stop your nagging eh
helluvanag furra man you
shut up and do as you are told
shuttit ndaywhit yurtellt
afore ah heid butt yi
criticising new labour
who do you think you are
whoojihink
learnt yur lessn eh
nae room fur dowt ma boy
nae room

palpitations, sore throat
anxiety and fear of death
come awkwardly while standing
on byres road waiting for a bus
buses are far too jerky
moving through the city
the orange train beneath
is too deep down
for breathing and lurking
and blurring vision
make it easy to catch
accidental death
at any time
pushing and pulling
at the end of a line...

never turned you into a landscape
never turned you into the law
never turned you out on the ocean
never turned you into a dream
never sucked your blood
never missed your heartbreak
never ran unruly through your world
never gave up on your future
never resented your past
never left you lovelorn
never let you starve
never forgot your birthday
never read your mail
never wanted to own you
never pissed on your cat
never bled on your carpet
never let your nose run
never slept with your friends
never set you on fire with matches
never kissed your cunt without asking
never twisted you round any fingers
never kicked away your chair
never left you in a waiting room
never kept your children alive
never decorated your bathroom
never sneezed in your face
never turned away from your kiss
never turned off your music
never turned sweet
never turned sour
never knew
never

never lived
never learned
never lost
never last
never laughed
never started
never saw
never stopped
never searched
never alchemy
never anything
never chemistry
never nothing
never knew
never thought
never prepared
never mourned
never missed
never managed
never heavy
never needled
never lactated
never came
never blamed
never honest
never fitted
never lied
never spewed
never cut
never ate shite
never turned to look
ever

25 TITLES FOR POEMS I'D NEVER WRITE

Can't stop laughing I'm bursting for a shite,
This is how it feels to write the sublime,
If the fishing is free it's not for me,
A long hymn to Temperance fair,
I want to be Harry Houdini,
The great generosity of Billionaires,
A special composition for your competition,
How I love my perfect teeth,
Popular fascists we all admire,
What sonnet work, is really What's on Network!
A sonnet to my haircut self-inflicted,
Sweet smell of my oxters – O how dear to me,
A welcome to all you debt-collectors and sheriffs,
Recovery for narcissists,
Taxing the wealthy cripples us all,
Insomnia my beautiful lover,
Low-paid catering job, oh how I love you,
Where's my fag my cock needs polished,
Low-paid cleaning job, I love you the best,
Keep up the good work all you racists,
Military spending keeps you healthy,
Give every Scot a gun,
Holmes and Watson were never ever gay,
The heterosexuality of Oscar Wilde,
The hairy parts of my Muse...

we are all made of outer-space

sun peeks

         onto green gleniffer braes
speed of light   travels faster than news
in 1790
        Sandy Wilson puffs on his pipe
collects whisky from his illegal still

of liberty, sun shifts higher—
warms rough-sodden-turf as it lilts up the sky
a whole lot slower than the speed of light—
takes hours to tumble down through the night—

our wee spinning globe
sees billions come and billions go
sailing in orbits of swirling dust—
we're all made of outer-space

a matter of matter changing form
a hundred million dollars
when Bowie was gone, told us
he'd been here, that

and a fistful of songs from the 1970s—
Sandy Wilson, ahead of Audubon, left us
The Birds of America,

some poetry books
a great-coat
and a haunfy o songs
    no bad gaun
for a man frae the braes o gleniffer—
        born June the 6th 1766.

155

alex harvey was our guide

this is not radio 4
it's verbal liberation
thundering through your door

this is not radio 3
it's a crazy gladness
flying into your tree

this is not radio 2
it's a sonic transformation
heading straight to you

this is alive, a real living space
this is street-life
it's a jungle full of grace

this is a man with stockings in his mouth
this is writing on our walls
with no need to head south

this is our voice, it's a glaswegian call
they think it's funny when you speak out
and it's funny when you fall

a cartoon hero with a dignified chant
with a crazy striped shirt
and a beatific rant

this is heh jimmy with a slice of jaques brel
it's a theatre of sound
you can touch, taste and smell

this is life uncovered as your feet take the floor
and your swimming up a river
you did not know you loved before

it's a tree and a fish
it's a bird and a bell
and aw that other crap that the tourist shops sell

it's laughter and hope and depression and death
it's a different holy book
it's your heartbeat and your breath

this is where they rob you
of your skills and your wealth
this is chain smoking life, it's inherent ill health

they will call you a nutter
they will call you off your fucking tree
if never the exploited nor exploiter shall ye be

this is radio without wage slaves
this is radio in your head
this is radio anything that you want to say instead

this is not radio 2
this is not radio 3
this is not radio 4

this is not radio 4
it's a live space
it's a door

it's a wide open door
it's a free and vibrant floor
this   is   not   radio   4

whose anonymous crimes are these?

who are you
who are you
tell me, please, who the fuck are you

did you die in 62
with shamrocks on your shoes
tell me, dæmon, who the fuck are you—

wise old woman
with thistles in her hair
gave us balloons to soar into the sky

dirty little man
with a spanner on his hip
left blind-innocence with a broken skull—

every trust was trampled the day you were born
jesus nor buddha could redemption bring
there was silence in the forest, filthy shadows on the streets
winter storms in radioactive zoos

be much better if you're dead
no more seedlings running red
from your squalid hands and monster rendezvous—

turns out you were a bomb from America
from India, Pakistan, France, Russia, Israel
you were China, North Korea and Great Britain too
tell me, dæmon, who the fuck are you

who are you
who are you,
please don't flash me once again,
please don't show me dæmon

who   the   fuck   are   you?

dare into dark

dare
to be different

dare
to be yourself

let
no gloomy bastard

oppress you

*

and when you pray
to your king everlasting

when you're in his arms
he doesn't give a damn

each day you wait
while his ignorance accrues

of your every pretty dream
and want and need

*

you're acutely aware
of being acutely aware

and still he doesn't care
about your economic mess

160

how to earn a crust
from the writing of yarns

and still you go on
alcoholic re-reformed

filling up your time
with sugar-cake and rhymes

say boo
to every evil in your twisted soul

and say goodbye
goodbye, goodbye

to all that
and all that's left as well

*

ideology
from the outside in

all a human construct
all a human construct

animal really
in its heart

*

and how do your eyes work
and what do you perceive

what can travel through
your iris densely-dark

little light vibrations
that tremble in your heart

in your heart
in your heart

waiting for a small war
to escalate and boom

send you to your tomb
where you'll sleep it off

sleep it all off
in his everlasting non-existent

king-like
bloody arms

John
Lennon's
Elbow
Transmits
Text Messages To Ma Brain

some people live in their cars
go about with sniper's eyes
keep their guns in sleeping bags
they're real regular guys

some folk live in the stars
shining bright with delusion
got control of their minds right now
but the only way to go is mad

some folk live in shanty towns
electricity's what they lack
they got no water to cook in
got whips biting into their backs

newspapers keep me warm at night
newspapers tell me the truth

ah got a bed of roses
ah got a bed of nails
ah got a bed of concrete and bones
got a sailboat with out any sails

and some folk
they can build their boats
and some folk
they can cook

others can cure cancer
and some folk
they write books

sad bastards   - with Mozart ringtones
sit on trains in trances destroying world peace

and
the quiet is far too quiet
and
loud is way too loud
and
young is always much too young
and
old is already dead dead old – pure dead but
brilliant old
by the way
and
middle aged is totally fucked
and
everybody's useless
except
mrs greedy and mr lust   - the thrusting
entrepreneurs

wah wwwaaaaahhhhhhh

(Scream: WWHHAAAAAAAAHHHH)

ahm oan msn
ahm oan lycos too
ahm oan cable, terrestrial, satellite and the broo
ahm oan dynamite without the mss
ahm oan ec-sta-cy
ahm oan bullets and Trojan horses
ahm oan LSD and GHB and horse pills that
keep yi gouched
ahm oan Moto sponsored movies
ahm oan Rubik's cube
ahm oan Diners Club and shrapnel
ahm oan change for the bus

ahm away to get a real joab noo
tell yi ma heid's totally fucked

coz

    John
        Lennon's
            Elbow
                Transmits

    Text Messages To Ma Brain

blues-waltz to nature

living

beats

working

I was doing the ShowerShave Et Cetera
and O, what a sweet old et cetera it is,
makes your face clean, your corruption unseen
beneath your hunger's luxurious dream —
forced to eat the shit called money
jester-servant not a master

how far can you see
from your narcissus tree
there's only a mirror, a mirror —
break out or move in
it's the time to begin, again
living, living, living

living
beats
working

any old time, now, shake yourself down
from that banker's big-money tree
pay all the bills for your ills —
Lucille has left home
you stand all alone
digging dark holes in the ground
it's an infinite job, no one to rob
no gem-stones reside in the dross,
and you take yourself down

deep into the ground,
wish you'd never sold your old cross —
just a servant not a master

humble you are, you look to the stars
as the earth tumbles down, tumbles down,
covers you up, living beats working beats death
and yet nothing, O nothing,
but the infinite order of auld mother nature
only that nothing, only that nothing,
only that nothing beats death

no symbol or song, no myth tall or strong,
but the process remains when you're gone,
just serving its will, it's invisible still,
can't get out of the narcissus tree,
your self was all you could see —
there are others, there are others

if you listen you can hear them
if you reach out you can touch them
if you breathe deep you can smell them
if you chew them you can taste them —
but your vision, your vision was cloudy
and you just could not glimpse the beyond

beats living
                    beats working
                                        beats death

beats living
                    beats working

beats

•••

doing the leg — an ephemeral dance

Nick Cave does the leg
Rudolph Nureyev does the leg
We all stand round, doing the leg
Eating cake, patiently, waiting for the bombs
We wonder at the meaning of the leg
But we are sleek smart Siamese cats
All the boys wear suits
All the girls wear hats
As [Insert U.S. President ?] lifts his simian finger,
                                    and points

at   disengaged ghosts
     fluorescent clouds
     burnt silver foil
     kleenex
     dvd-hi-fi-junk
     Skittles and M n Ms
     MacHeath sings
     a knife in his throat
     gurgling blood
     Glasgow weeps
     over its pearly young
     enamel stained teeth
that
     extra-whitening Michael Jackson
     treatment can't remove or
     ever turn back the atomic clock
     shimmering sun transforming shafts
     of pastel dream light out the window

of the Polmont train, walking
up the blustery platform
just at nightfall
the wind so strong it blows
your cranium clean apart
showing an audience of stars
Slim Whitman singing *Ten Guitars*
(if ever he did)

too sad
and beautiful moustachioed women
who kiss the lips of
ancient peacenik-hippy-boyfriends, girlfriends,
say goodbye to *Ruby Tuesday*, destroyed in blue obscurity,
just like you and me
aching for some good old home-made charity, certainty,
to know
when it's safe to go to the shops

as scientists assemble nano-machines,
they can rebuild us from the inside
if we can afford it
cryogenically freeze the head
of every US President, alive or dead,
Mount Rushmore can all be put back
the way it was before the nutters invaded (Iraq?)
we sit at home with ice-cream cones, waiting,

waiting

waiting for the van to sink into a coma, searching,
for daylight-loving insect life
absorbing scag from the marrow of bones, refreshing,—
sending all the aristocrats
to their aristocratic rest homes —
MacHeath's face in a broken mirror, smiles
his white-pearly-teeth remain unstained

> officials come in,
> they work for someone PRIVATE
> but keep up PUBLIC ORDER

while

Nick Cave does the leg
Robert Burns does the leg
We all dance round, doing the leg
Eating ice-cream, patiently, waiting for the bombs
We wonder about the meaning of the leg
But we are sleek smart Siamese cats
All the boys wear suits
All the girls wear hats
As The U.S. President lifts his simian finger
$\qquad$ and points at all the maps